Level -1

Contemporary Underground Stations of the World

Lisa Baker

Level -1

Contemporary Underground Stations of the World

BRAUN

CONTENTS

PREFACE

The oldest subways were built as an urban extension of the intercity railway network. In the 19th century, the largest railway stations were built on the edge of the city and often served only one direction, like the Gare de l'Est in Paris. As the number of passengers increased, train connections in the inner city became necessary. The first subway in London went into operation in 1863; connecting Paddington, Euston and King's Cross underground and using wooden wagons pulled by a... steam train! The line was continuously expanded despite the dense smoke and steam in the stations and tunnels, not to mention in the train wagons, and in 1880 the inner circle was completed – built entirely to the north of the Thames. Marc Brunel's tunnel (1835–1843), which stretched beneath the Thames and connected the city quarters of Rotherhithe and Wapping, was also used by a steam train, despite originally being built for use by pedestrians and horse-drawn vehicles. This served as a connection to the South London Line, drawing the individual lines together to form a network.

The Athens & Piraeus Railway Company soon followed in London's footsteps, and Istanbul also began constructing an underground route for horse-drawn omnibuses (funicular tunnel, 1875). However, the idea of an underground public transport system only really made a breakthrough when trains were powered by electricity. In 1879 Werner Siemens presented an electric-powered train at the Great Industrial Exposition in Berlin and in 1881 he opened the first electric tramway in Berlin-Lichterfelde. Following Siemens's plans, the first electric subway line was built in Budapest in 1896 and London also began using electric trains in 1905.

An important milestone in architectural history that took place in around 1900 was the construction of the Métropolitain in Paris. In 1897 and in preparation for the World Fair in 1900, the city of Paris and the French government agreed on the construction of six subway lines, after the idea of building a metro network had been on the cards for almost 30 years. This network was 65 kilometers in total and work began on line 1 in 1898 – stretching from Porte de Vincennes to Porte Maillot. However, the network was not completed for the World Fair in April 1900, but was actually finished in July. It transported four million passengers during its first six months of operation. Charles Garnier, the architect who also built the Paris Opera, declared that Paris residents would only accept the Métro in their city if it were presented as a work of art and not simply a functional construction. After a competition to select the design was held and failed to select a winner, young architect Hector Guimard was commissioned based on his successful design for the Castel Béranger. He fused the rational design of Eugène-Emmanuel Viollet-le-Ducs with the Victor Hortas's organic esthetic. By 1914, a total of 141 entrance pavilions and cast iron arches in abstract floral shapes were constructed. The design was also economical because numerous elements were prefabricated. Only a few of the large stations still remain today (Abesses – formerly the Hôtel de Ville, and Porte Dauphine, both from 1900; as well as Châtelet, 1901). The two largest stations were both dismantled in 1925 and 1962. The Paris Métro has the highest user satisfaction level in the world in comparison to other local public transport networks.

In Asia, the Tokyo subway network went into operation in 1927 and even today has the highest number of passengers in the world – along with the Moscow subway. However, the Tokyo subway barely meets demand and "pushers" are employed to help optimally fill the carriages during rush hour.

Despite all these developments, elevated railways that were built on stilts and stretched through the historical old towns dominated until the First World War. It wasn't until after 1945 that city planners began to view subways as a way to remedy inner-city traffic problems, while trams were removed as they were seen as causing a disruption to the flow of traffic. The most important subway network at that time was built in Moscow, where Josef Stalin constructed numerous subway stations known as "palaces of the working class". During the 1930s, the stations were built in the Art Déco style, while those constructed after the Second World War were examples of Social Classicism. In both cases, the stations were decorated in historical style and expensive materials were used in the construction (Image: Komsomolskaya Station by A.V. Shchusev, 1952). Even today, the Moscow stations clearly show this tradition, although the details have become more modern and abstract. The choice of materials and the basic fundamental shapes are still very much connected to local architectural history.

Triangeln Station is an underground railway station in the heart of the city of Malmö, one of three new stations on the six-kilometer City Tunnel which links Malmö with the Öresund Bridge and Copenhagen. The number of travellers per day is around 37,000, making Triangeln Station Sweden's third busiest railway station. Smoothly integrated into the urban environment, the station is within easy walking distance from many destinations. Triangeln Station is located at a depth of 25 meters and is designed as a bored rock cavern. The shape of the station hall is a result of the technology used to create the rock cavern. To clearly signal the underground station in the cityscape, the two entrances have a uniform glass pavilion design and same construction principles, but with differing geometric shapes.

TRIANGELN STATION
MALMÖ, SWEDEN

Architects: Sweco Architects, KHR arkitekter
Artists: Gunilla Klingberg and Christian Partos
Location: Saint Johannesgatan and Smedjegatan, Malmö, Sweden
Completion: 2010
Gross floor area: 9,500 m²
Number of public levels: 3
Number of platforms: 1
Number of passengers/day: 37,000

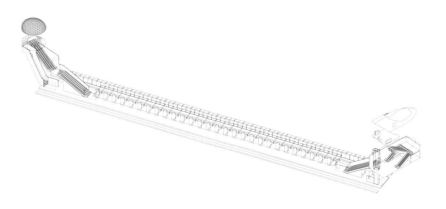

"All this began in the Metro (first-class) with the phrase:
'l'homme que j'étais, je ne le suis plus.' " –
Henry Miller, American writer

MÓRICZ ZSIGMOND KÖRTÉR STATION
BUDAPEST, HUNGARY

This new metro station is located in one of Budapest's busiest transport hubs and connects to an underpass completed a few years ago. The platform is approximately 20 meters below ground level and can be accessed via escalators and elevators from two sides. Construction progressed according to the 'Milano method', where final works on the ground floor and the station's construction underground were done at the same time. The character of the new station is determined by huge interior spaces, concrete surfaces and leaning reinforced concrete walls. The station's translucent building on the ground floor, containing elevators and a canopy, draws the natural light inside the interior platform spaces. Most of the concrete surfaces appear gray, although some are painted different colors.

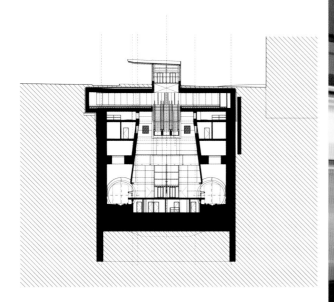

Architects: Gelesz and Lenzsér
Location: Móricz Zsigmond körtér, Budapest, Hungary
Completion: 2014
Gross floor area: 1,200 m^2
Number of public levels: 2
Number of platforms: 1
Number of passengers/day: 15,000
Additional functions: retail

The Budapest Metro is not only the second oldest metro system in the world
but also the only one that has been designated
an UNESCO World Heritage site.

Located in a densely developed area in Nuremburg, the functional above-ground sections of the Maxfeld underground stations are also an interpretation of the wider location. In order to have a minimal effect on the appearance of the street, the two entrances/exits are designed as slab-like layers, similar to earth thrown up by shifting fault lines. These connect the daylight area above with the underground world below, and are designed to be experienced as a separate spatial entity. The design of the walls below ground is inspired by the location and features quotes from German poets, after whom the nearby streets are named. As a reference to the German poet and author Goethe, part of his work is featured in the design of the station hall.

MAXFELD
SUBWAY STATION
NUREMBERG, GERMANY

Architects: Haid + Partner, Architekten + Ingenieure
Location: Goethestraße, 90409 Nuremberg, Germany
Completion: 2008
Gross floor area: 1,800 m²
Number of public levels: 2
Number of platforms: 1
Number of passengers/day: 10,000

The New York City subway operates 468 stations,
more than any other metro system in the world.

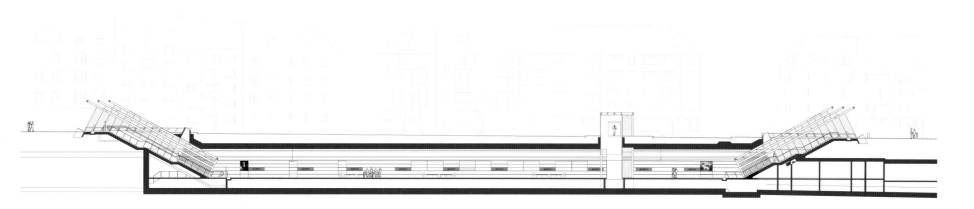

Architects: Gerber Architekten
Location: Umm Al Qura Road, Makkah, Saudi Arabia
Completion: 2022
Gross floor area: 81,450 m²
Number of public levels: 1
Number of platforms: 6
Number of passengers/day: max. 140,000 during the Hajj
Additional functions: retail

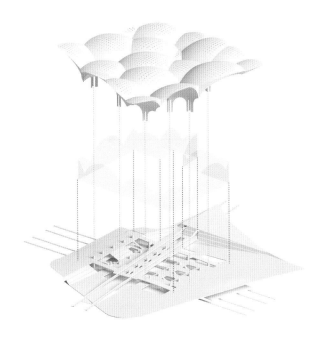

HARAM INTER-MODAL STATION
MAKKAH, SAUDI ARABIA

Haram Intermodal Station will be the main station of the new metro system in the Holy City of Makkah and shall serve as a design guideline to all other underground stations in the city. Several overlapping domes of various diameters span the large station concourse and create vaults, which terminate in mid-air or are taken into the ground by way of slender columns. The dome surfaces are covered with glass mosaics of different shades of white, incorporating Islamic ornamentation. Skylights of dichroic glass, which become bigger towards the top of each dome, create atmospheric light reflections inside the station. The large forecourt slopes gently down into the main station to create an interchange level for the three crossing metro lines.

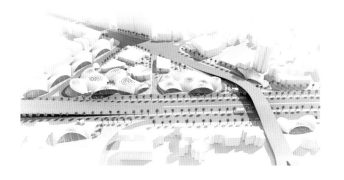

Only two cities on the African continent currently operate metro systems: Cairo and Algiers.

ÜBERSEEQUARTIER SUBWAY STATION
HAMBURG, GERMANY

The entrances guide commuters down into an underwater world. The Überseequartier station focuses on the physical character of the element water, with its density, permeability and surface tension. The spatial geometry spreads outwards over the ticket booths and distribution levels and allows views of the platforms – the central train station hall. It is here that the spatial impression reaches its culmination. The appearance of the station is characterized by its technical esthetic, which relates to the topic of water with its minimalist colors and soft reflections. The walls and ceiling of the platform hall depict an artificial underwater world.

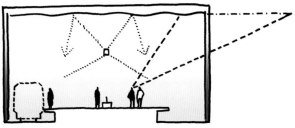

Architects: netzwerkarchitekten
Location: Überseequartier, HafenCity, Hamburg, Germany
Completion: 2012
Gross floor area: 8,460 m²
Number of public levels: 3
Number of platforms: 1
Number of passengers/day: 35,000

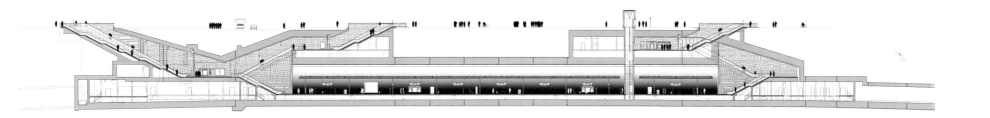

"The only way to be sure of catching a train is to miss the one before it." – Gilbert K. Chesterton, English writer and poet

Architects: Palatium Studio
Location: Kálvin tér, Budapest, Hungary
Completion: 2014
Gross floor area: 6,900 m²
Number of public levels: 5
Number of platforms: 1
Number of passengers/day: 120,000
Additional functions: retail

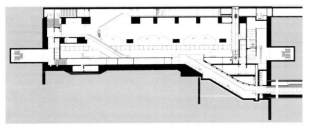

KÁLVIN TÉR
STATION
BUDAPEST, HUNGARY

Kálvin tér station on the line M4 accommodates two underground lines under the busy urban square. It was constructed with cut and cover technology that provided the opportunity to create a large and undisrupted open platform space. The extensive use of rough exposed concrete helps to give the entire design the desired unity. Horizontal supports function as main structural elements and have a characteristic curved form. The elevator tower, escalators and huge ventilation ducts with their glazed smoke-curtains are decisive elements of the spatial composition. A graphic mosaic design decorates the entrance of the station. The colorful atmosphere of the tunnel towards the platform of M3 line responds to the architectural world of both the old and new lines.

All but six of the world's busiest train stations are located in Japan.

The innovative and dramatic design of the Museum station on the Toronto Transit Commission's University Subway Line re-imagines the station platform as a hypostyle hall supported by archeologically inspired elements. The designs of the five columns are based on artifacts from the Royal Ontario Museum and the Gardiner Museum, located above the station. The columns are repeated throughout the station's platform representing Canada's First Nations, Ancient Egypt, Mexico's Toltec culture, China's traditional culture and Ancient Greece. The new station design helps to orient subway passengers to the city above, providing visual clues about the activities on street level. The project successfully combines functionality, esthetics and culture.

TORONTO MUSEUM SUBWAY STATION
TORONTO, CANADA

Architects: Diamond Schmitt Architects
Location: 75 Queen's Park, Toronto, ON M5S2C5, Canada
Completion: 2008
Gross floor area: 2,700 m²
Number of public levels: 1
Number of platforms: 1
Number of passengers/day: 8,500

"Buy the ticket, take the ride." —
Hunter S. Thompson, American author and journalist

Architects: Metrogiprotrans
Interior designers/artists: N. Shumakov, A. Nekrasov, G. Mun
Location: Novoyasenevsky prospekt, Moscow, Russia
Completion: 2014
Gross floor area: 11,000 m²
Number of public levels: 3
Number of platforms: 1
Number of passengers/day: 30,000

BITCEVSKY PARK STATION
MOSCOW, RUSSIA

The focus of Bitcevsky Park station is a large colorful panel displaying a combination of graphics that adds a strikingly colorful accent to the space. The lights are located in extended niches that resemble huge raindrops reflecting the sunlight. The arched ceiling is asymmetrical and carries out two tasks: It offers the necessary structural support and provides light. The colorful wall panels contrast the white ceiling; this has the added advantage of automatically drawing the eye towards the graphics.

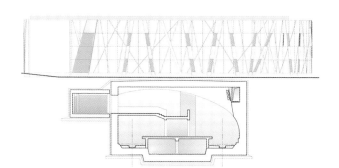

The Moscow Metro runs a train called the "Aquarelle Train"
that displays replicas of famous works of art for its passengers.

DRASSANES
SUBWAY STATION
BARCELONA, SPAIN

The design of this metro station was constrained by two factors: the restricted space available and the nature of the existing components. As a solution, the architects based their design on the interior appearance of a train carriage. The gleaming white of the station mimics the sparse interior of a high speed train, stripping away all unnecessary elements and emphasizing the location. The criss-crossing illuminated lines in the black ceiling are an abstraction of a network of train tracks crossing over each other. The green columns and mosaic-like wall panels in other areas add a touch of color to the design.

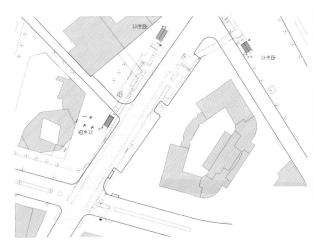

Architects: ON-A
Location: Avinguda Drassanes, 08001 Barcelona, Spain
Completion: 2009
Gross floor area: 1,500 m²
Number of public levels: 2
Number of platforms: 2

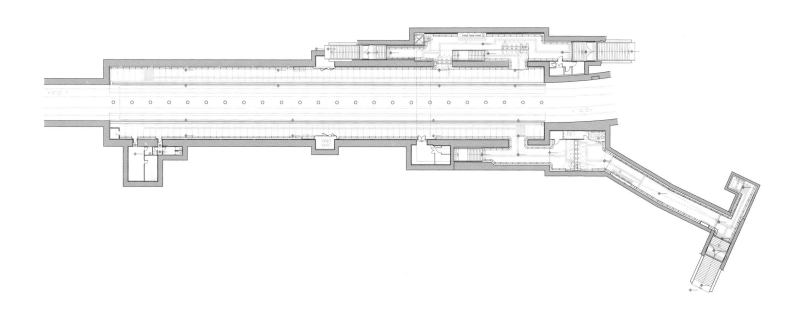

The Arsenalna metro station in Kiev, Ukraine is the world's deepest
underground station at 105.5 meters.

Architects: HPP Architects
Location: Willy-Brandt-Platz, 04109 Leipzig, Germany
Completion: 2013
Gross floor area: 8,273 m²
Number of public levels: 2
Number of platforms: 2

CITY TUNNEL LEIPZIG / LEIPZIG MAIN STATION SUBWAY
LEIPZIG, GERMANY

One of the largest infrastructure projects to be undertaken in Leipzig, this project was officially inaugurated in December 2013 with the opening of the City Tunnel. HPP Architects, who were also responsible for planning the renovation of the main train station, were commissioned to design this station. Two large two-story atria allow views of the various levels and also permit better control of the area as it is easier to see what is happening on the platform. The materials used for the walls include stone and glass, and these were also used in the two atria. The platforms and connecting areas are optically drawn together to create a coherent whole that welcomes commuters above ground and accompanies them all the way to their train.

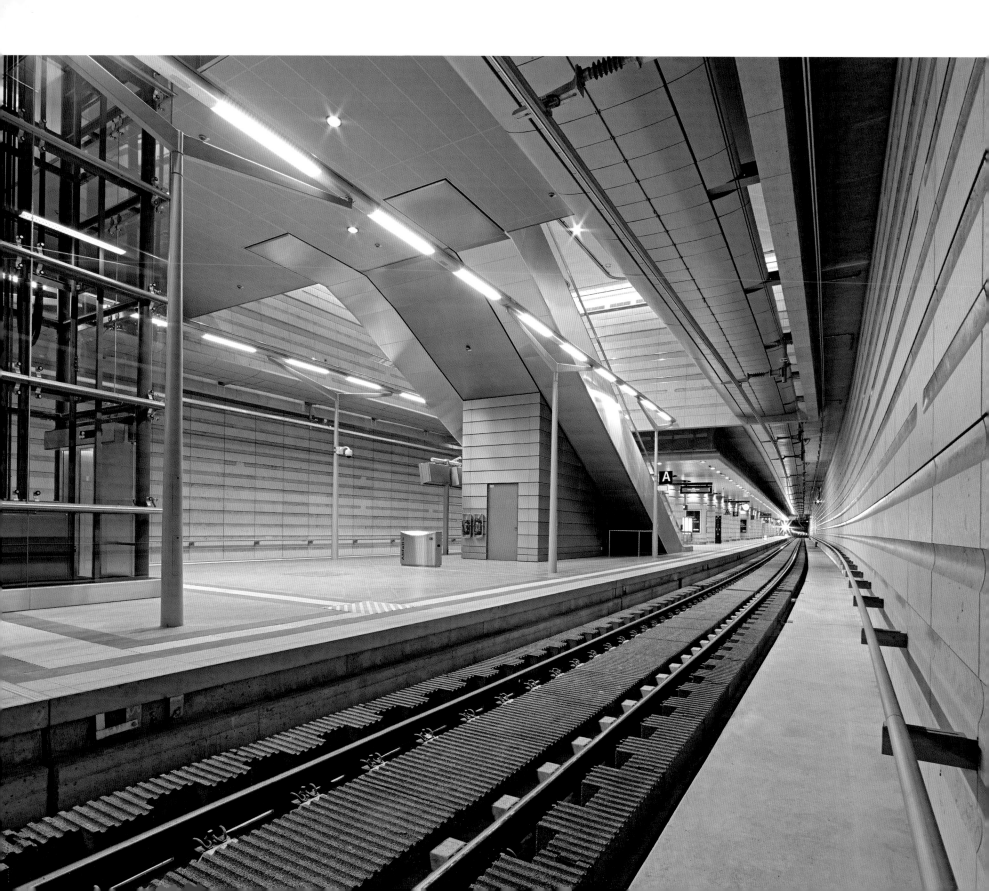

"If you board the wrong train, it is no use running along the corridor
in the other direction." –
Dietrich Bonhoeffer, German theologian and Nazi dissident

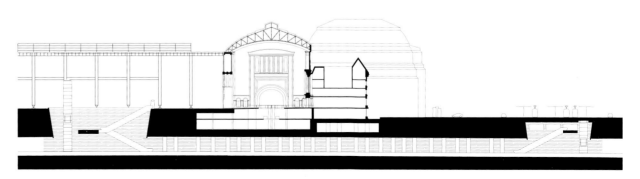

This design not only revitalizes the location, but also preserves its valuable trees and connects the market hall and the square. Mining methods were used in the construction in order to maintain the existing trees. Two aboveground edifices were built: the escalators are housed in one, while the lifts and stairways are located in the other. The two visible reinforced concrete skeletons stand back-to-back, their cantilevered roofs pitch towards each other. A pool is located between the two buildings, in the middle of the square.

RÁKÓCZI TÉR STATION
BUDAPEST, HUNGARY

Architects: Budapesti Építőművészeti Műhely
Location: Rákoczi square, 1084 Budapest, Hungary
Completion: 2014
Gross floor area: 7,010 m²
Number of public levels: 3
Number of platforms: 2
Number of passengers/day per line: 100,000
Additional functions: parking lot, reconstruction of public place

"People who want to understand democracy should spend less time in the library with Aristotle and more time on the buses and in the subway." –
Simeon Strunsky, American essayist

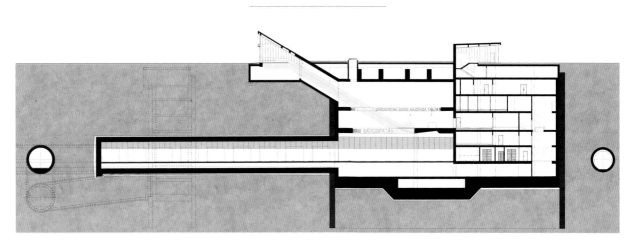

Architects: Dominique Perrault Architecture
Location: Piazza Garibaldi, Naples, Italy
Completion: 2014
Gross floor area: 13,120 m²
Number of public levels: 4
Number of platforms: 2
Number of passengers/day: 18,000
Additional functions: public space, commercial gallery,
cinema, parking lot, access to train station

PIAZZA GARIBALDI
NAPLES, ITALY

Dominique Perrault was commissioned by the Metropolitana di Napoli to redesign the Piazza Garibaldi and build an accompanying subway station. The chance to design a new metro station provided the architect with the opportunity to reform the urban space, creating a location full of vitality and characterized by the fragmentation of the pedestrian spaces. A huge gallery has been inserted into the ground and the underground network is permitted to surface at certain points, drawing light into the depths. High metal 'trees' rise out of the ground to support the roof.

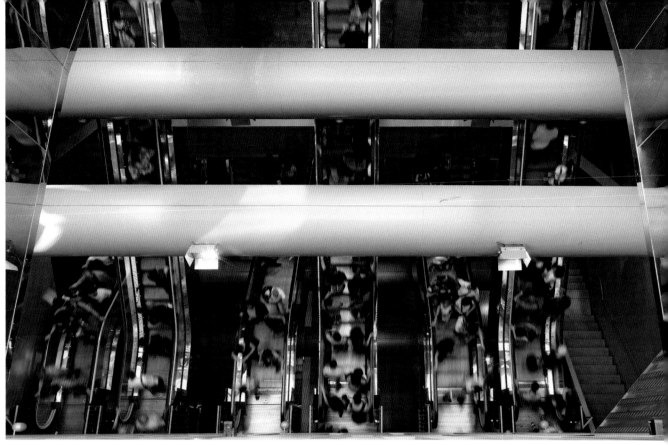

"I'm not a car guy. The subway gets me where I need to go efficiently and cheaply, and I don't worry about traffic." –
Joe Scarborough, American news presenter

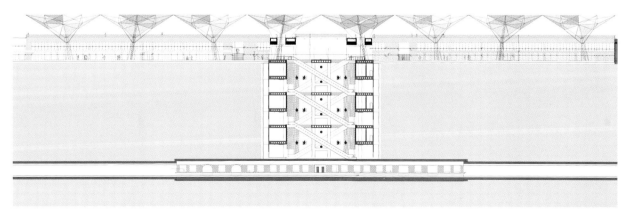

HEUMARKT
SUBWAY STATION
COLOGNE, GERMANY

The north-south subway line in Cologne will not only improve traffic flow in the city center, it is also an impressive architectural construction. In order to give each station a distinctive appearance, eight different architects were commissioned to individually plan the eight stations of the line; thus, each station has its own individual signature. Despite this, a unified design gives each station the same quality. Various kinds of concrete have been used, combined with terrazzo or hard-aggregate screed flooring and the same escalator model and glass elevators were also used throughout. The security of the passengers and orientation were also top priorities. Each of the stations is as transparent as possible. Daylight has been integrated into the design concept and creates a unique atmosphere.

Architects: Prof. Ulrich Coersmeier
Location: Heumarkt, 50667 Cologne, Germany
Completion: 2013
Gross floor area: 6,131 m^2
Number of public levels: 3
Number of platforms: 2
Additional functions: retail

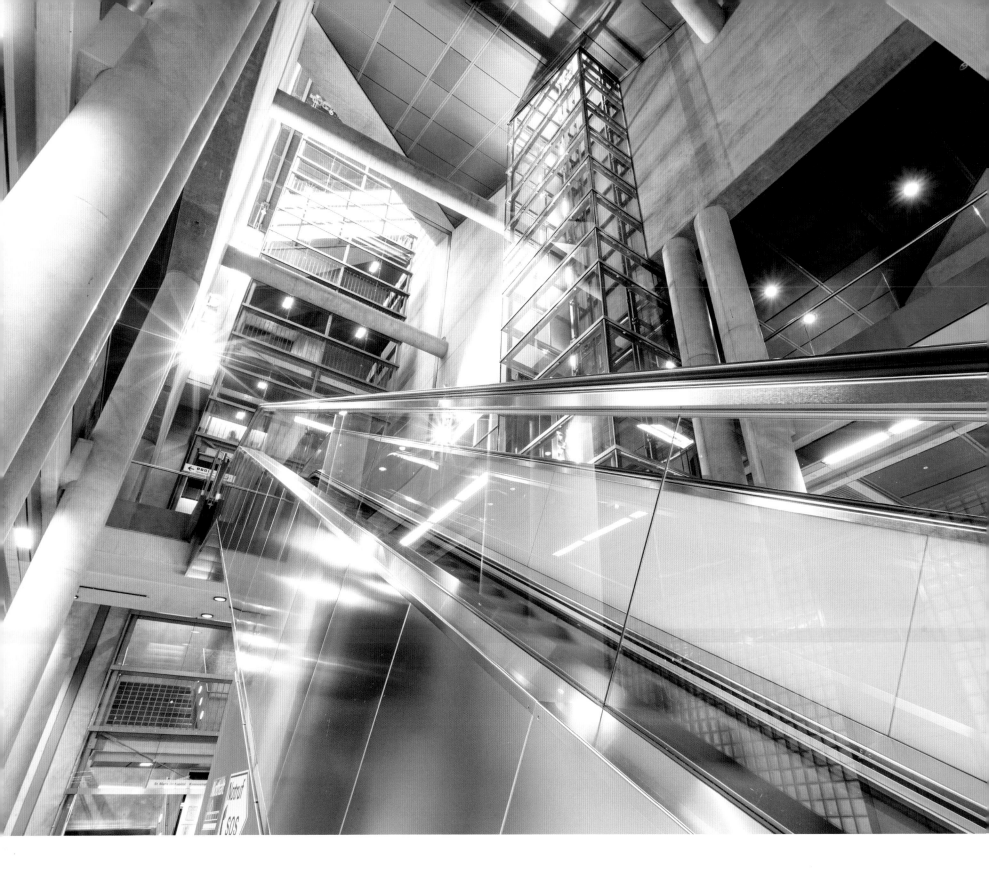

"You can't understand a city without using its public transportation system." –
Erol Ozan, researcher and author

The Olaya metro station reinterprets the Arabian desert landscape and thus establishes a dialogue between tradition and future. The site of the Olaya metro station is located in the center of Riyadh's rapidly developing Olaya district. The station will become the most important metro station in this district and is thus designed as an iconic landmark that can be seen and accessed from each direction. The sculptural form creates a park, which gradually rises upwards in gentle waves to become the roof of the Olaya station. This dune park will cater for the pressing need for more green urban space in Riyadh. Contemporary and minimalistic design is combined with traditional and regional elements, while light and sound installations underpin the concept and create a unique atmosphere.

OLAYA METRO STATION
RIYADH, SAUDI ARABIA

Architects: Gerber Architekten
Location: Olaya St, Al Wurud, Riyadh 12216, Saudi Arabia
Completion: 2019
Gross floor area: 92,700 m²
Number of public levels: 5
Number of platforms: 4
Additional functions: retail spaces, food courts

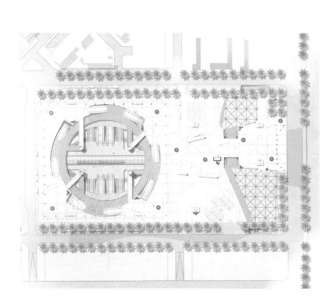

"What was once underground is now coming to the surface." —
Gavin Bryars, English composer and double bassist

U2 PRATERSTERN SUBWAY STATION
VIENNA, AUSTRIA

The fundamental design idea for the U2 line was the consequential development of the existing Vienna systems. In contrast to other large cities, the guiding theme was the coherent design of the entire line, including the materials, spatial development and colors used. Numerous new stations on the U2 line all share the same floor surface design, platforms, stairs, lifts and ceilings. The wall cladding responds to the specific situation of each station. For example, an important design medium for the Praterstern station is the use of natural light to illuminate the platforms. This increases the spatial effect and also aids orientation.

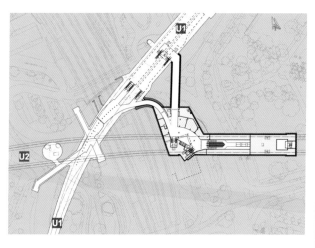

Architects: Architekt Gerhard Moßburger
Location: Praterstern, 1020 Vienna, Austria
Completion: 2008
Gross floor area: 16,465 m²
Number of public levels: 4
Number of platforms: 2
Number of passengers/day: 103,900
Additional functions: retail passage

The Pyongyang Metro in North Korea uses former Berlin subway cars.

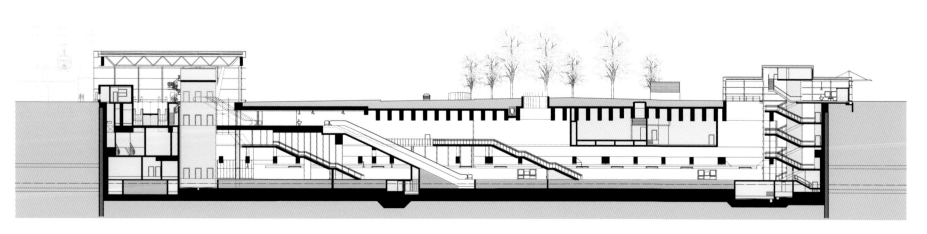

Architects: AMC – Andrzej M. Choldzynski
Location: Plac Wilsona, Slowackiego Street, Warsaw, Poland
Completion: 2005
Gross floor area: 8,970 m²
Number of public levels: 2
Number of platforms: 1

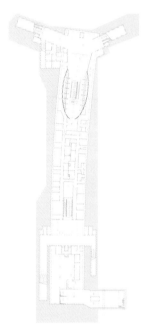

PLAC WILSONA A-18 SUBWAY STATION
WARSAW, POLAND

Plac Wilsona A-18 subway station is located in the heart of Żoliborz. Consistency between the design of reinforced concrete structure, technology and function form a coherent architectural whole. The intention was to create a space of peace and tranquility, monumentality, contrary to the hectic hustle and bustle usually associated with subway stations. The heart of the underground part of the station is the space beneath the reinforced concrete oval dome. Changing colors illuminate this concrete shell: dawn, midday and evening light. The dome creates a mega-acoustic structure which absorbs the noise of passing trains and users. Exits from the station are also an example of the symbolic language prevalent throughout the design.

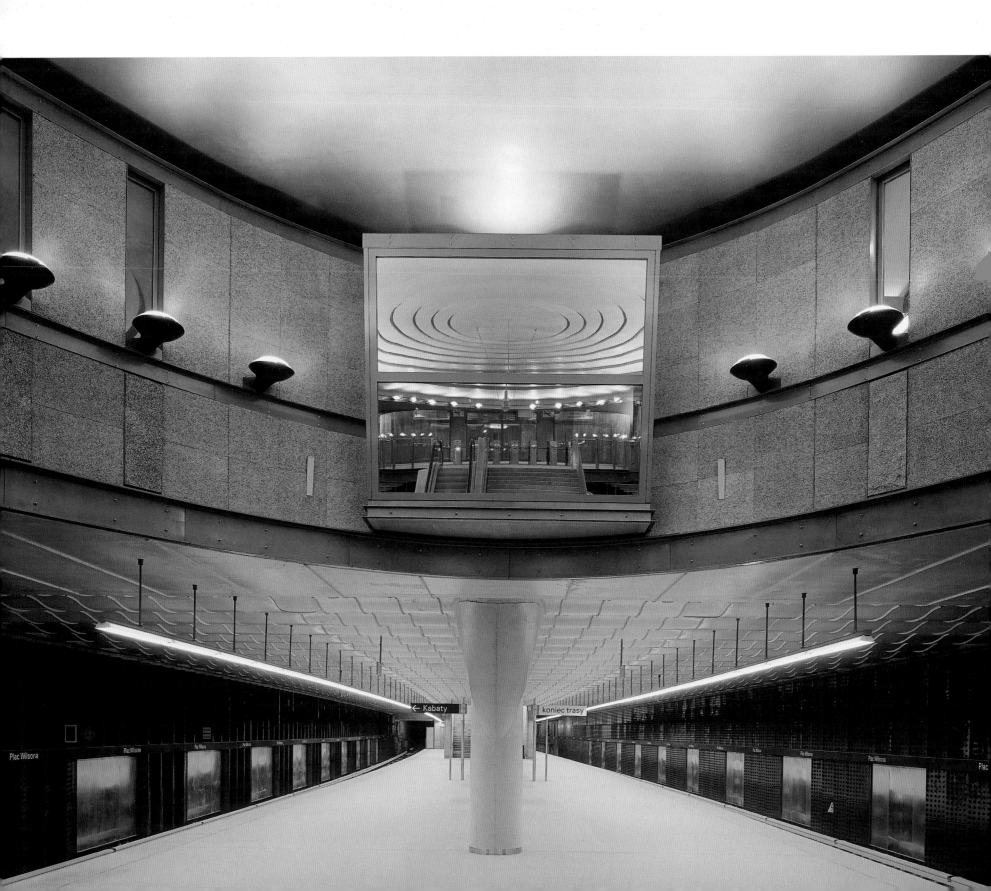

The London Underground was opened in 1863 and is the world's oldest metro system.

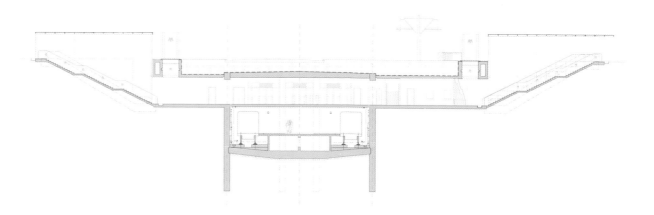

Chlodwigplatz is one of the most important transport nodes in Cologne's Südstadt. The simple yet elegant entrances to the underground station are characterized by glass elevators and stairways. The central distribution level has an elliptical floor plan that responds to the geometry of the public square above. The stairs and escalators transport commuters to the train platforms below. The staircase to the north leads over a small elliptical-shaped pedestal and ends directly in front of the Severinstor gate. Despite the complicated construction, the structure has been reduced to a simple spatial geometry. Large sections of the concrete construction have been realized with a surface of exposed concrete. The carefully executed finishes are in line with the minimalistic design concept.

CHLODWIGPLATZ SUBWAY STATION
COLOGNE, GERMANY

Architects: Schaller/Theodor Architekten
Lighting design: Kress & Adams Atelier für Tages- und Kunstlichtplanung
Location: Chlodwigplatz, 50678 Cologne, Germany
Completion: 2014
Gross floor area: 4,500 m²
Number of public levels: 2
Number of platforms: 2
Number of passengers/day: 15,000
Additional functions: connecting station to above ground lines

The Shinjuku Station in Tokyo is the world's busiest station,
used by an average of 3.6 million people per day.

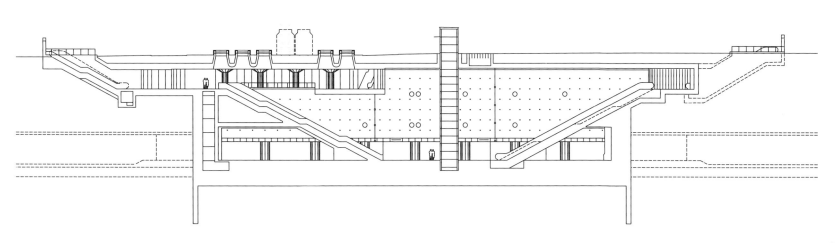

TOTTENHAM COURT ROAD CROSSRAIL STATION WESTERN TICKET HALL
LONDON, ENGLAND

Built over 100 years ago as two separate tube stations, Tottenham Court Road was not designed to cope with the almost 150,000 passengers passing through the sation now every day. With the expected rise in passenger numbers interchanging between London Underground services and Crossrail in 2018, the existing station is being upgraded to meet the expected rise in demand for this key central London station for years to come. Alongside the upgrade of the existing tube station, Crossrail is building a new station. A new street level western ticket hall will be constructed at Dean Street, with the station box continuing five levels below ground at a depth of around 25 meters, providing access to the new Crossrail platforms.

Architects: Hawkins\Brown
Location: Dean Street, London W1D, England
Completion: 2018
Gross floor area: approx. 6,000 m²
Number of public levels: 3
Number of platforms: 2 crossrail platforms
Number of passengers/day: 150,000

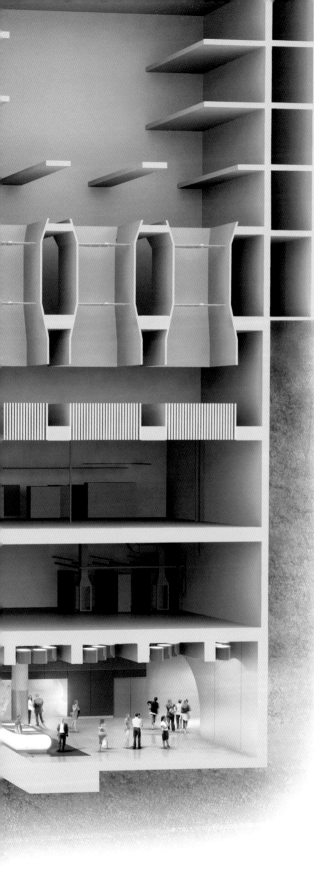

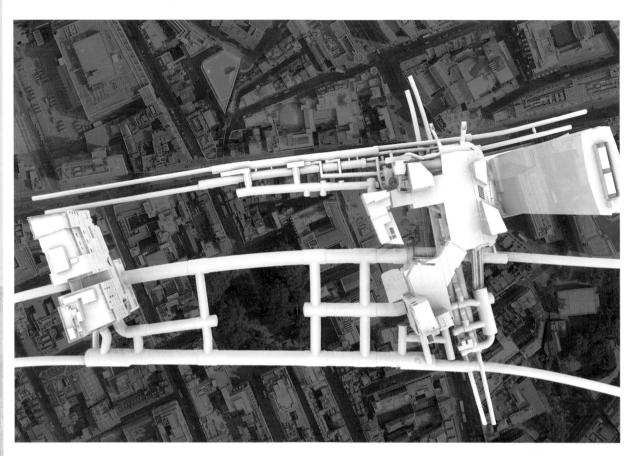

When the Circle Line in London opened in 1884, the Times described it as 'a form of mild torture, which no person would undergo if he could conveniently help it'.

Architects: Hassell
Location: Epping / Macquarie University /
Macquarie Park / North Ryde,
Sydney, Australia
Completion: 2009
Gross floor area: 5,000m²/station
Number of public levels: 3
Number of platforms: 2
Number of passengers/day: 12,000

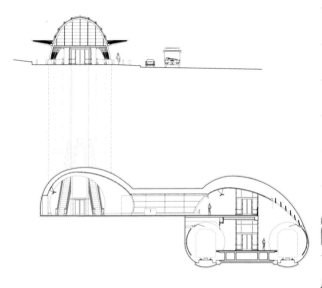

EPPING TO CHATSWOOD RAIL LINK
SYDNEY, AUSTRALIA

The organization of these underground stations is simple and legible; a sequence of spaces which calibrate the journey into another realm. A dramatic entrance cavern, augmented by deep penetration of natural light generates a sense of calm, clarity and timelessness befitting the stations' importance as contemporary public buildings. The design presents a new sustainable typology with ticketing, amenities and management located deep underground. The station livery presents as a refined industrial language appropriate to its time and place. In the stations the air is clean, the temperature mild and the acoustics crisp. The new stations demonstrate that travel by rail can be enjoyable, comfortable and uplifting; an urbane experience each day in a global city.

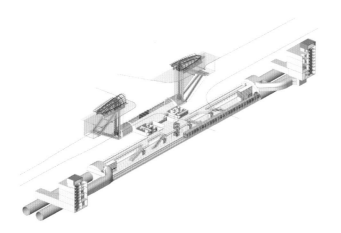

"If I ever have to stop taking the subway, I'm gonna have a heart attack." –
Edward Norton, American actor and film director

KAULBACHPLATZ SUBWAY STATION
NUREMBERG, GERMANY

The Kaulbachplatz subway station is located to the north of Nuremburg's Old Town in the Gärten an der Veste quarter. The design of the entrances and exits establishes a dialogue between organic elements and the floral Jugendstil of the district. Slim concrete walls flank a sloping glass roof that opens out to the street above, creating a light and welcoming entrance and exit situation. The elliptical openings between the two dark concrete walls allow a view of the street. The transparent glass construction allows a glimpse of the sky and helps to draw a wealth of daylight deep into the underground station. Underground, the walls comprise white structural concrete featuring filigree structural matrixes that depict artworks from various artists, after whom the neighboring streets are named.

Architects: Haid + Partner, Architekten + Ingenieure
Location: Schweppermannstraße, 90408 Nuremberg, Germany
Completion: 2011
Gross floor area: 1,700 m²
Number of public levels: 2
Number of platforms: 1
Number of passengers/day: 10,000

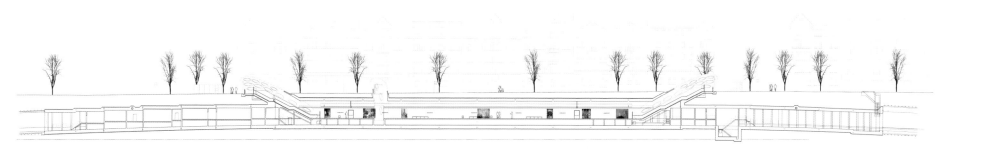

"The underground of the city is like what's underground in people.
Beneath the surface, it's boiling with monsters." –
Guillermo del Torro, Mexican film director and novelist

Architects: Metrogiprotrans
Interior designers/artists: N. Shumakov, V. Volovich,
D. Khokhlov, I. Jumagulov
Location: Yasenevaya street, Moscow, Russia
Completion: 2012
Gross floor area: 13,900 m^2
Number of public levels: 3
Number of platforms: 1
Number of passengers/day: 29,000
Additional functions: transition to the station Krasnogvardeyskaya

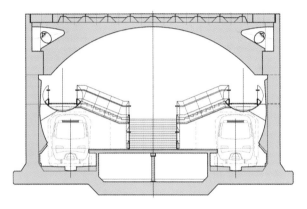

ZYABLIKOVO STATION
MOSCOW, RUSSIA

The Lublinsko-Dmitrovskaya segment of the Moscow metro line from Maryino station includes three stations – Borisovo, Shipilovskaya and Zyablikovo. The most important aspect of the design was to create an underground architecture with unified design elements. The small-scale architecture elements located above ground include ventilation ducts, elevators, entrance and exit pavilions. The light niches inserted into the design give the arch an almost sculptural appearance. The colors used for the stations are a combination of black, gray and white.

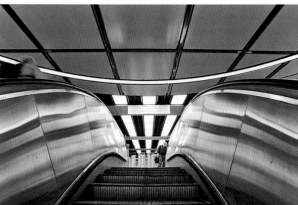

Metro-2 is the informal name of an apparently secret metro network in Moscow that supposedly runs parallel to the Moscow Metro.

The Olympia Shopping Mall subway station is located in the north of Munich at the point where the lines U1 and U3 cross. In order to achieve a variety of different atmospheres in the two overlapping platform halls, the walls of the U1 are clad with folded, matte stainless steel panels, interrupted every eight meters by shining mirror plates. On the U3 platform, the walls are clad with pyramid-shaped metal panels. The design was inspired by the desire to give the station a technical appearance to suit its function, while also creating a varied play of light and shadow. The folded walls on the U1 line and the pyramid-shaped cladding on the U3 create very different reflections, not just of light but also of the passengers and trains.

OLYMPIA SHOPPING MALL
SUBWAY STATION
MUNICH, GERMANY

Architects: Betz Architekten
Location: Pelkovenstraße / Hanauer Straße, 80993 Munich, Germany
Completion: 2008
Number of public levels: 3
Number of platforms: 2
Additional functions: park and ride

"I have against me the bourgeois, the military and the diplomats, and for me, only the people who take the Metro." —
Charles de Gaulle, French president

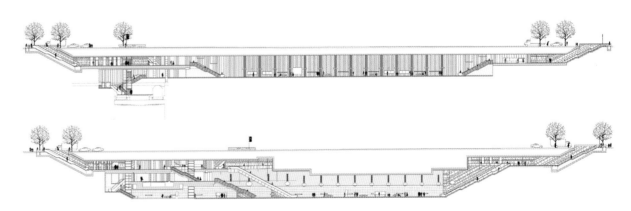

Architects: BDP
Location: Whitechapel, London, England
Completion: 2018
Number of public levels: 2
Number of platforms: 6

WHITECHAPEL STATION
LONDON, ENGLAND

This new and improved design for Whitechapel Station includes a whole host of upgrades, which will benefit passengers and local residents. The plans incorporate daylight, improving the passenger experience while enhancing the historic features and unique personality of the existing station as much as possible. The main entrance has been reinstated on Whitechapel Road, and a walkway alongside the concourse will provide a new public pedestrian route from the entrance on Durward Street to Whitechapel Road. The access and ventilation shafts around the station have been designed to minimize impact on local residents. When Crossrail opens in 2018, Whitechapel station will become an important transport hub connecting the new line to the District, Hammersmith & City and Overground lines.

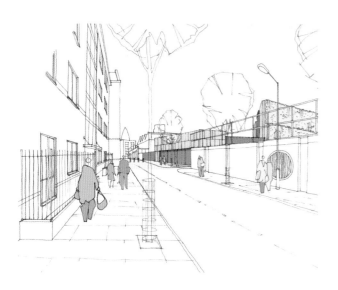

"Anything is possible on a train: a great meal, a binge, a visit from card players, an intrigue, a good night's sleep, and strangers' monologues framed like Russian short stories." –
Paul Theroux, American travel writer and novelist

The Leipzig Markt metropolitan rail station is located directly under the market, and at the intersection of a crossroad that was once at the heart of the historical city layout. The station is connected to Leipzig's extensive underground network. The effect of the proportions and dimensions of the arched station hall is increased by the rhythm of the white concrete ceiling trusses and the large number of extremely slim steel pipes. These formulate a basilica-like interior and define the waiting areas. The spatial organization is characterized by bridges, stairs and the elevator tower. Steel loggias in the façade mediate between inside and outside.

MARKT STATION
LEIPZIG, GERMANY

Architects: ksw kellner schleich wunderling architekten + stadtplaner
Location: Markt 1a, 04109 Leipzig, Germany
Completion: 2013
Gross floor area: 4,700 m²
Number of public levels: 3
Number of platforms: 2
Number of passengers/day: 41,000
Additional functions: historic entrance hall

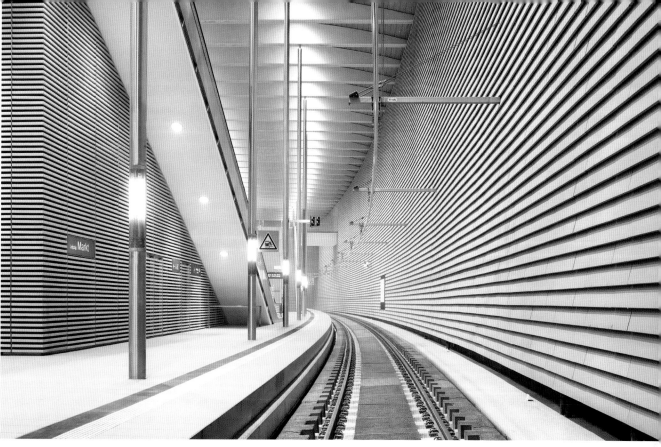

The longest metro tunnel in the world is also the longest railway tunnel.
It stretches over a distance of 60.4 km and is located in Guangzhou, China.

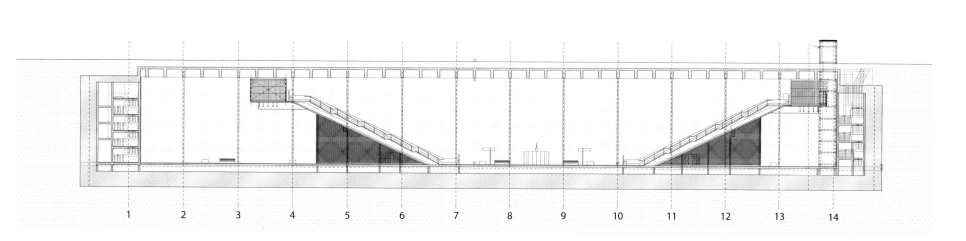

1   2   3   4   5   6   7   8   9   10   11   12   13   14

BIKÁS PARK STATION
BUDAPEST, HUNGARY

Following a national competition in 2004, Palatium Studio built up a network of architecture offices to define a common architectural language for the design of Budapest's new M4 metro line, although the ten stations were designed individually. Bikás Park station is one of the stations designed by the studio itself: Situated in the corner of a large park, it opens towards the sky with a glazed dome, illuminating the main access to the platform. The dome is a slim lightweight structure, based on a grid of triangles, some of them solid for shading and creates an interplay of light and shadow in the depths of the station. Graphic elements, flowers on fiber-concrete cladding and flying seeds on glazed smoke-shields decorate the walls of the station, echoing the impressions of the park.

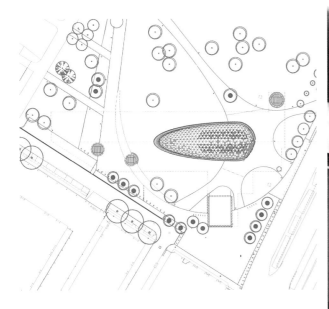

Architects: Palatium Studio
Location: Bikás Park, Budapest, Hungary
Completion: 2014
Gross floor area: 6,500 m²
Number of public levels: 3
Number of platforms: 1
Number of passengers/day: 40,000

The no-pants subway ride is a tradition in New York
that takes place every year in January.

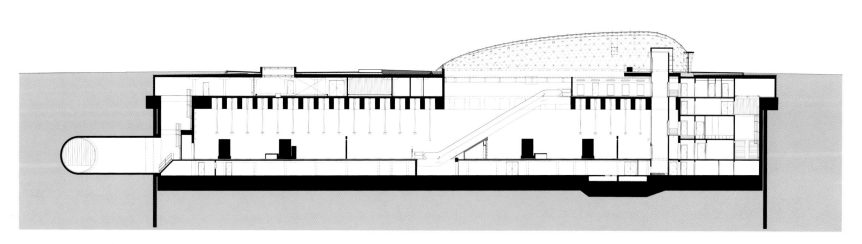

Architects: Max Dudler
Location: Wilhelm-Leuschner-Platz, 04107 Leipzig, Germany
Completion: 2012
Gross floor area: 5,679 m²
Number of public levels: 2
Number of platforms: 2

WILHELM-LEUSCHNER-PLATZ SUBWAY STATION
LEIPZIG, GERMANY

This metropolitan railway station on Wilhelm-Leuschner-Platz/ Platz der Friedlichen Revolution is one of four stations serving the new Leipzig City Tunnel. The character of the platform hall is defined by elements of backlit glass blocks along the walls and ceilings. The apparently never-ending repetition of constructional elements along the gently curving, well-lit platforms increase the perception of the dimensions inside this large construction. All furnishings inside the station are geometric concrete sculptures arranged along the central platform. The design of the two entrances contrasts the transparent appearance of the platform hall. As soon as one enters the underground realm, the staircases are made of concrete, attaching seamlessly onto the platforms to form one long band.

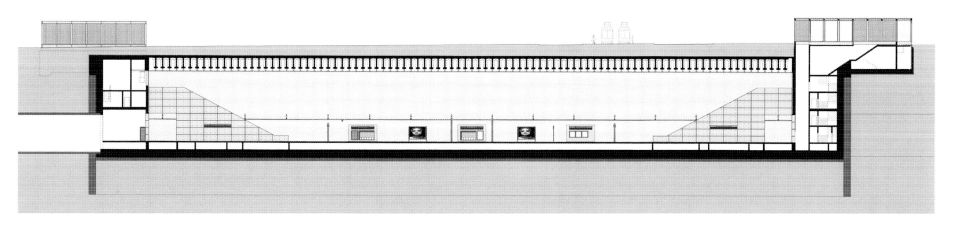

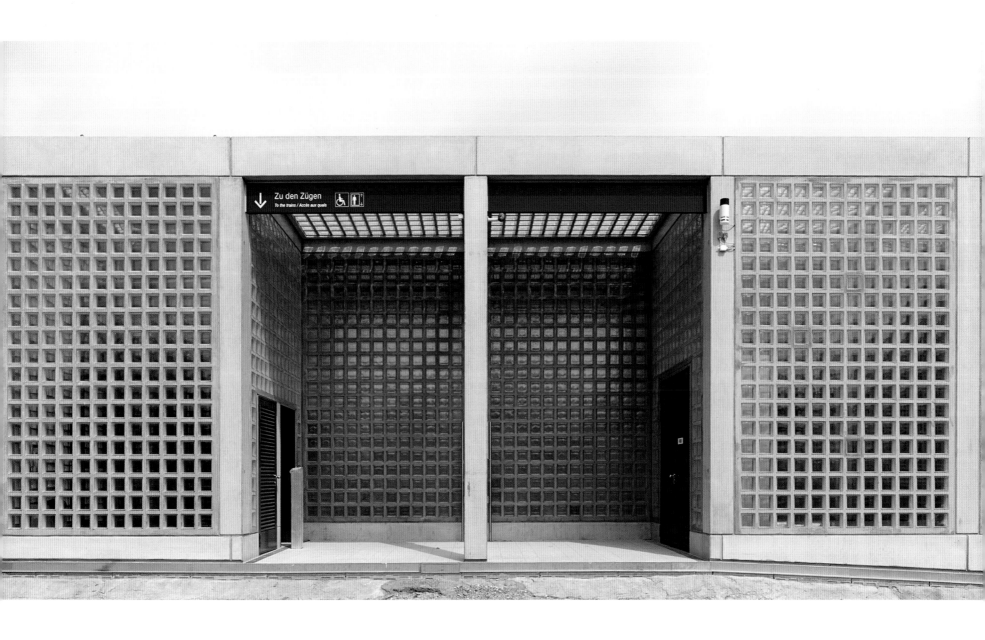

"The ability to master physical communication – the ease with which people can move freely and in a civilized manner – is essential to the future of our cities; and the architecture of this kind of infrastructure is critical to urban development." – Norman Foster, English architect

Architects: AMC – Andrzej M. Choldzynski
Location: Jana Kasprowicza, Bielany district, Warsaw, Poland
Completion: 2008
Gross floor area: 8,173 m²
Number of public levels: 2
Number of platforms: 2

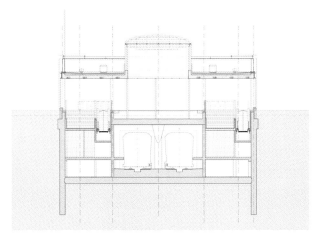

WAWRZYSZEW A-22 SUBWAY STATION
WARSAW, POLAND

The Wawrzyszew A-22 subway station is located between the park and forest greenery in the vicinity of the housing estates built during the communist era. The historical Bielany district is situated next to the station, and is based on the idea of the garden city for workers during the interwar period. The entrances to the subway are free-standing pavilions made of glass, steel and graphite-gray brick. Steel trellises on top of the pavilions are covered by greenery rising along the glazed walls. Mega-skylights on the roof of the pavilions draw daylight inside. The space is designed to slow down the traffic rhythms and perception, calming communication and the roar that comes from the continuous movement of trains.

"One thing about trains: It doesn't matter where they're going.
What matters is deciding to get on." –
Conductor in the film "The Polar Express"

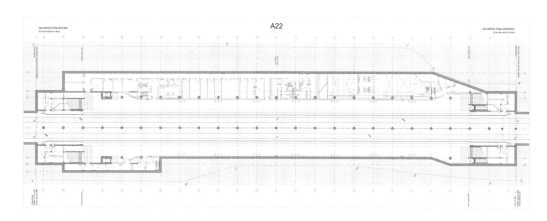

Located at a depth of 84 meters, Victory Park station is the deepest of the Moscow subway. It is cross-platform junction, where two subway lines meet. The decoration of the station is devoted to the victories of Russian armies in two wars: The war with Napoleon in 1812 and World War II. The pictures at the ends of both platforms describe these events. The architecture of the station is characterized by its classical style. Escalators 126 meters in length unite the platforms with the station above, connected by an underground passage with an exit on Kutuzovsky Prospekt.

VICTORY PARK STATION
MOSCOW, RUSSIA

Architects: Metrogiprotrans
Interior designers/artists: N. Shumakov, N. Shurygina, A. Orlov, A. Nekrasov, Z. Ceritelli
Location: Kutuzovsky Prospekt, Moscow, Russia
Completion: 2003
Gross floor area: 39,500 m²
Number of public levels: 3
Number of platforms: 2
Number of passengers/day: 43,000
Additional functions: transition from two lines of Moscow's Metro

The Moscow Metro is commonly regarded as having
the most beautiful stations in the world.

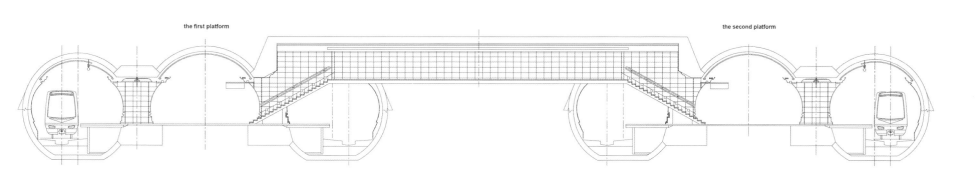

the first platform

the second platform

Architects: Hentschel - Oestreich
Location: Pariser Platz, 10117 Berlin, Germany
Completion: 2009
Gross floor area: 5,200 m^2
Number of public levels: 2
Number of platforms: 1

BRANDENBURGER TOR
SUBWAY STATION
BERLIN, GERMANY

The geometry of this station is defined by the densely developed situation at the entrance/exits, the curving railway and the existing metropolitan railway line located parallel to this underground. The unified wall design of large shell limestone panels and the continuous flooring surface of light terrazzo develop the heterogeneous spatial organization into a unified whole. The platform level is characterized by black supporting columns and a suspended luminous ceiling. An exhibition focusing on the Berlin Wall and Brandenburger Tor is integrated into the wall cladding around the rear wall and the staircases.

"Even if you're on the right track you'll get run over if you just sit there." –
Will Rogers, American actor and social commentator

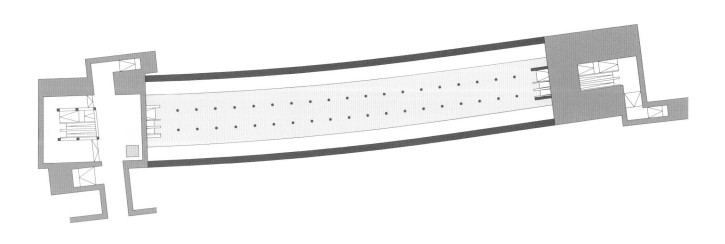

LONDON CROSSRAIL
VARIOUS LOCATIONS, ENGLAND

Grimshaw forms part of the multi-disciplinary C100 consortium for the Crossrail project. Taking passenger experience as the key driver, the consortium is designing the architectural components that will be used throughout the platform and tunnel environments to create an integrated line-wide identity. The Crossrail project comprises 40 stations and will link Maidenhead and Heathrow in the west, to Shenfield and Abbey Wood in the east via 21 kilometers of new tunnels under central London. It is estimated that around 200 million passengers will travel on Crossrail each year. Simple, forward-thinking and intuitive passenger environments have governed the design, which will be completed in 2019.

Architects: Grimshaw
Engineers: Atkins
Location: various locations, London, England
Completion: 2019

"There's something about the sound of a train that's very romantic and nostalgic and hopeful." – Paul Simon, American musician

Architects: Pahl + Weber-Pahl
Location: Willy-Brandt-Platz, 44787 Bochum, Germany
Completion: 2006
Gross floor area: 5,100 m²
Number of public levels: 3
Number of platforms: 1
Number of passengers/day for entire network: 397,000

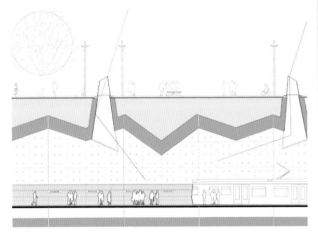

RATHAUS-SÜD STATION
BOCHUM, GERMANY

Bochum's city center was gray and desolate, with streets that had been devaluated by heavy traffic. This was the starting point for the design of an underground railway intersection and above-ground redesign project. Opened in 2006, this design has created an unmistakable, unusual space characterized by the effect of light and glass. 13 prismatic volumes of pre-crushed sandwich glass penetrate the streetscape and draw daylight into the station below. This develops a link between the areas both above and below ground. Furthermore, the long station walls are also constructed of layers of backlit glass. These glass walls help to absorb some of the noise thanks to slits between the glass panels and the hollow space behind.

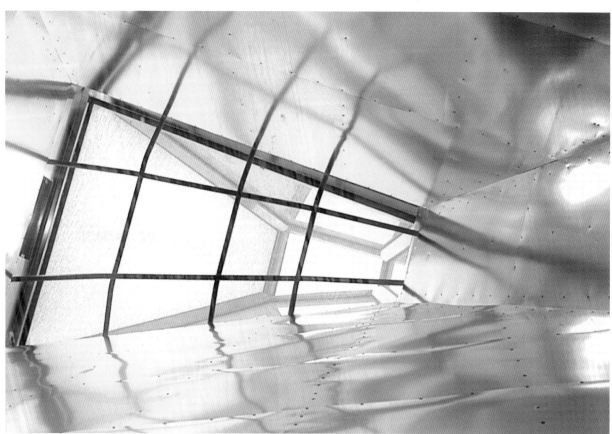

The largest and most complex underground station in the world is
Châtelet – Les Halles located in Paris, France.

Stadium MRT Station in Singapore is designed to recreate the delight of Victorian train stations in the golden age of rail travel. It serves the surrounding entertainment and leisure facilities as well as the nearby East Coast condominiums and is designed for large crowd surges. The design evokes the experience of a natural canyon – a slice in the earth between two stratified walls. The walls are clad in a single aluminum extrusion that is designed to be installed in four different orientations, giving infinite variety to the wall. The platform is clad in reflective colored blue and green quartzite and backlit glass panels, a cool and shimmering 'ice cave' beneath the large linear skylight.

STADIUM MRT STATION
SINGAPORE, SINGAPORE

Architects: WOHA
Location: 3 Stadium Walk, Singapore 397692, Singapore
Completion: 2008
Gross floor area: 9,204 m^2
Number of public levels: 2
Number of platforms: 2

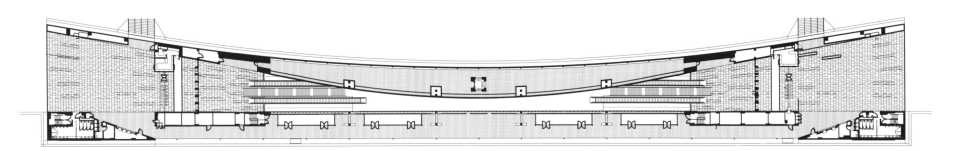

"Urban design as a discipline barely exists in most American and Canadian cities. In Singapore, there are innovative transportation strategies at work." – Moshe Safdie, Israeli/Canadian/American architect

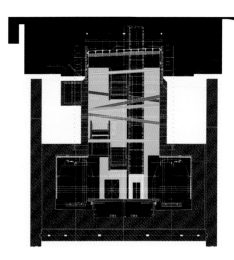

Architects: Peter Kulka
Location: Bayerischer Platz, 04103 Leipzig, Germany
Completion: 2013
Gross floor area: 2,500 m²
Number of public levels: 2
Number of platforms: 2

BAYERISCHER BAHNHOF METROPOLITAN RAILWAY STATION
LEIPZIG, GERMANY

The Bayerische Bahnhof station is located to the south-east of Leipzig's Old Town. It was built in the 1840s and was the oldest remaining railway terminus in Germany. The railway system on the historical railway lines was still in operation until just a few years ago. A city tunnel is currently being built in Leipzig within the framework of the reorganization of the regional and metropolitan railway traffic. The new station is part of this project. The above-ground element of the entrances and exits are deliberately modest, so as not to draw attention away from the historical main entrance. The impression of the underground station is defined by the voluminous skylights above the escalators, which draw a wealth of light onto the platforms. The apparently random colored poles function as both constructional elements and light sources.

The word "metro" actually comes from an abbreviated form of the "Paris Metropolitan" — the shortened name of the company which originally operated most of Paris' network: La Compagnie du chemin de fer métropolitain de Paris.

The interior of the CERIA station was shaped to reflect the dynamics of transportation. The design process was dominated by various constraints, such as accommodating the already existing passageways in one building. The centralization of the previously isolated elements produced the structure's unique form, adapting to the spaces it shelters within. The building rises to provide access to the depths and then continues up into the air, becoming a roof and a formal entrance that draws customers into the station, before plunging down again to guide the passenger flows.

CERIA-COOVI STATION
BRUSSELS, BELGIUM

Architects: GS3 partners architects
Location: Chaussée de Mons, 1070 Brussels, Belgium
Completion: 2014
Gross floor area: 250 m²
Number of public levels: 2
Number of platforms: 1

"I never travel without my diary. One should always have something
sensational to read in the train." –
Oscar Wilde, Irish author

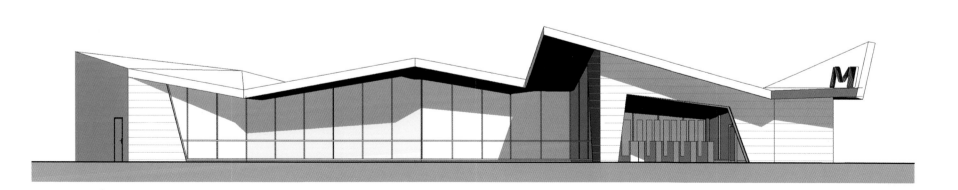

Architects: Auer Weber
Location: Central Station, 80331 Munich, Germany
Completion: 2014
Gross floor area: 8,400 m²
Number of public levels: 2
Number of platforms: 2
Number of passengers/day: 200,000
Additional functions: retail

MUNICH
MAIN STATION
DISTRIBUTION LEVEL
MUNICH, GERMANY

The distribution level of this underground station, opened in 1980, has been renovated and redesigned without disrupting the day-to-day operation. The design is based on the principle of a 'street as meeting place'. The kiosks have been removed and the shops arranged solely on the west side, in the direction of the main train station. An illuminated wall with integrated ticket machines, info points, and telephones is located on the opposite side. The wall changes color depending on the time of day. LED lighting is integrated into the ceiling, while the light granite paving is equipped with a striking way-finding system. White glass tiles reinforce the underground station's clear and light character.

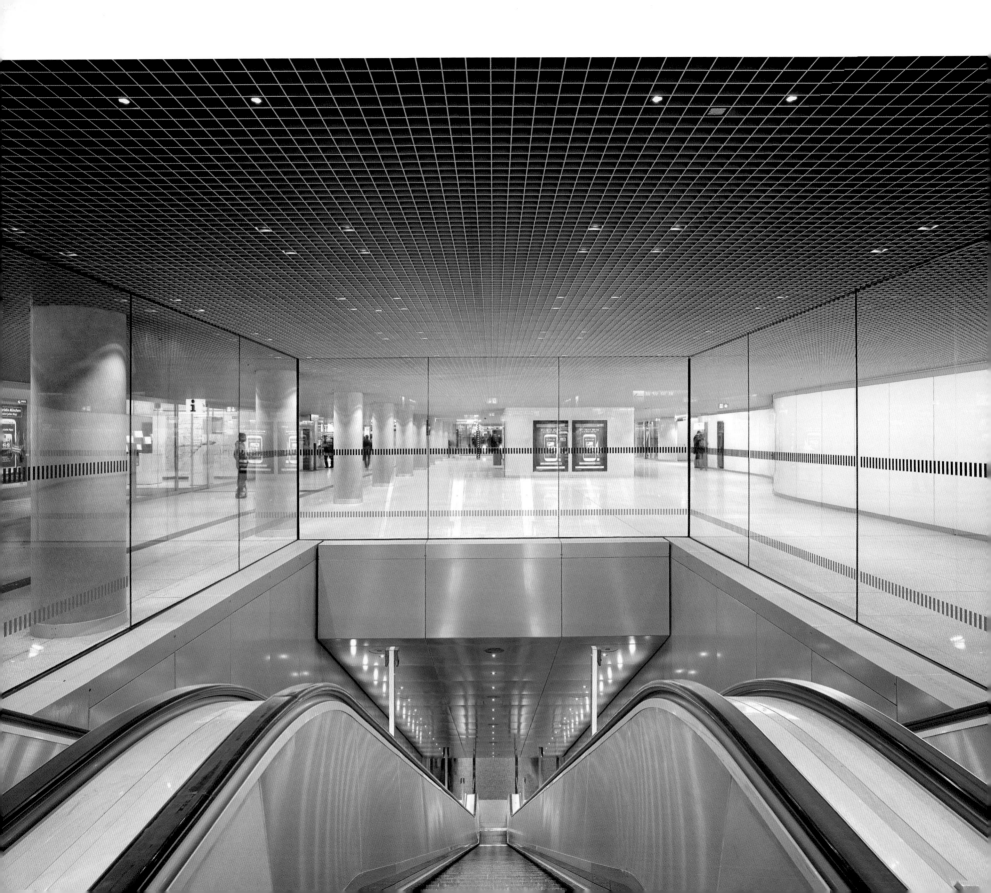

"Neither a wise man nor a brave man lies down on the tracks of history to wait
for the train of the future to run over him." –
Dwight D. Eisenhower, president of the United States

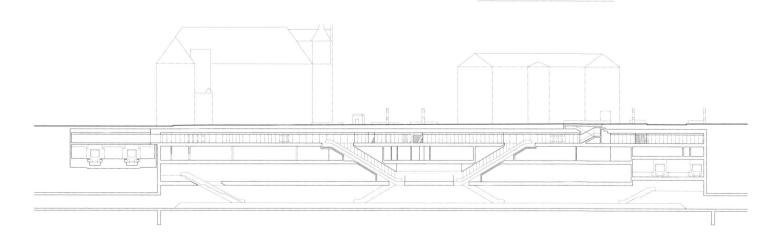

The disciplined spatial concept for this underground station creates a location that concentrates solely upon the spatial effect, while the barrel vaulted ceiling has been left largely untouched. The glass floor serves to illuminate the station, while at the end a powerful red wall features an illuminated yellow cross that establishes a connection between the overlying crossroads and the station, defining the border of subterranean cavity. A concept by Düsseldorf artist Eva-Maria Joeressen and a sound installation by composer Klaus Kessner were also integrated into the design from the very early stages. The design of this station demonstrates a disciplined architectural language that doesn't draw attention away from the spatial impression of the space itself.

LOHRING
SUBWAY STATION
BOCHUM, GERMANY

Architects: Rübsamen+Partner Architekten und Ingenieure
Artists: Klaus Kessener (sound installation "U-Musik"),
Eva-Maria Joeressen (installation 102 m ü NN)
Location: Steinring / Lohring / Wittener Straße, 44789 Bochum, Germany
Completion: 2006
Gross floor area: 1,800 m²
Number of public levels: 3
Number of platforms: 1
Number of passengers/day: 3,200

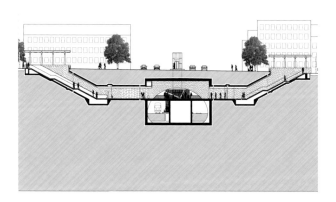

In the Moscow Metro the upcoming station is announced
by a male voice on inbound trains to the city center,
and by a female voice on outbound trains.

SZENT GELLÉRT TÉR STATION
BUDAPEST, HUNGARY

Szent Gellért tér station is one of the deepest stations on the M4 line; it is composed of a cut and cover box and tunnels. The box is supported by levels of reinforced concrete beams, producing a structure similar to a net or skeletal system. The architectural and structural concept is based on a random beam grid and the underground texture and construction system were compatible without compromising the often volatile and changing conditions of the planning and building processes. The main front of the box is a concrete wall covered with corten steel, while the tunnels have a curved cross section. The walls and the columns are covered with mosaic tiles reflecting the Zsolnai ceramic tiles of the nearby Gellért hotel.

Architects: sporaarchitects
Location: Szent Gellért tér, Budapest, Hungary
Completion: 2014
Gross floor area: 7,100 m²
Number of public levels: 3
Number of platforms: 1
Number of passengers/day: 15,000

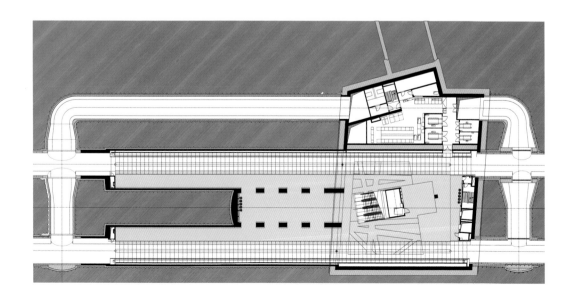

"One never need leave the confines of New York to get all the greenery one wishes —
I can't even enjoy a blade of grass unless I know there's a subway handy or a record
store or some other sign that people do not totally regret life." —
Frank O'Hara, American writer, poet and critic

Architects: GS3 partners architects
Location: Avenue des Amandiers, 1020 Brussel, Belgium
Completion: 2014
Original completion year and architect: 1998/Groupe Structures
Gross floor area: 180 m²
Number of public levels: 2
Number of platforms: 1

ROI BAUDOUIN
SUBWAY STATION
BRUSSELS, BELGIUM

This upgrade program for the Brussels metro involved the creation of a surface entrance structure housing the new access control point and a lift. Following the principle that a metro station has no pre-established architectural vocabulary, the design uses highly contemporary, free flowing forms that seek to express the dynamic nature of this mode of transport. The building also marks the entrance to the underground world. The entrance hall acts as a funnel directing passengers into the depths of the station. This is lined with a covering of aluminum composite that changes color with changing lighting levels.

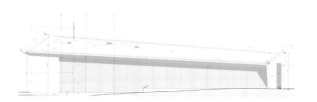

"A nickel will get you on the subway, but garlic will get you a seat." –
American proverb

URUGUAI STATION
RIO DE JANEIRO, BRAZIL

North of Rio de Janeiro, Uruguai Station occupies an old parking area for trains, known as "Rabicho da Tijuca". The conversion into a platform area required that the grid of 138 existing concrete columns was replaced by 23 steel columns located at the center of the platform, with six structural brackets branching out of each column. Technical rooms, elevators and stairs were positioned on both ends of the platform, where the original structure was preserved. The mezzanines are located on both ends of the station, below street level. The accesses, located on Conde de Bonfim Street, were executed in metallic sheet piles, minimizing expropriations and reducing costs. Lighting and ceiling solutions have played a great role in reducing structural irregularities.

Architects: JBMC Arquitetura & Urbanismo
Location: Rio de Janeiro, Brazil
Completion: 2014
Original completion year and architect: 1989 /
Companhia do Metropolitano do Rio de Janeiro
Gross floor area: 13,775 m²
Number of public levels: 3
Number of platforms: 1
Number of passengers/day: 36,000
Additional functions: underground parking garage

"I love New York, I love the smell of New York ... I love the subway." –
Harold Ford, Jr., American politician

Architects: Palatium Studio
Location: Fehérvári út, Budapest, Hungary
Completion: 2014
Gross floor area: 6,800 m²
Number of public levels: 5
Number of platforms: 1
Number of passengers/day: 50,000

ÚJBUDA-KÖZPONT STATION
BUDAPEST, HUNGARY

Újbuda-központ station is located on the M4 line and clearly represents the general idea behind the design of the stations on this line. The passenger areas are large and open, providing more than enough space for passengers. Situated in a relatively narrow street, the entrance area is marked by the escalators and elevators positioned at the very end of the platform. The horizontal supports are decisive architectural elements that help to define and characterize the space. Additional light is provided by the special sculpted cast-glass wall at the end of the platform. Above, the vibrant metal-wire surface of the acoustic ceiling is illuminated by colored lights. The standard furnishing elements on the central line of the platform are decorated on this station by special glass textile panels.

"Sometimes that light at the end of the tunnel is a train." –
Charles Barkley, American basketball player

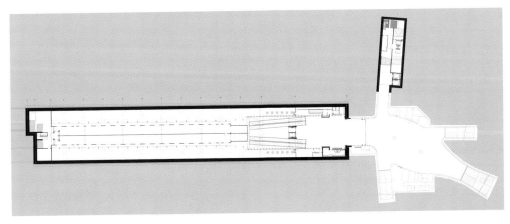

HAFENCITY
UNIVERSITY
SUBWAY STATION
HAMBURG, GERMANY

This design reacts to the location and identity of Hamburg's Hafencity: to the colors of the brick façades and steel ship hulls, which change depending on the season and time of day; to the powerful crane systems, and the shipping container modules. The building shares a dialogue with the maritime environment. The Hafencity atmosphere is created by the materials used on the walls and ceilings and the suspended light container in the station itself. The cladding used on the walls and ceiling comprises pre-treated panels of oxidized steel. Each of the panels differs slightly from the next thanks to their individual surfaces. The 12 lighting elements suspended above the platform offer a large and dynamic lighting solution that creates a simple yet impressive atmosphere and responds to the location and function.

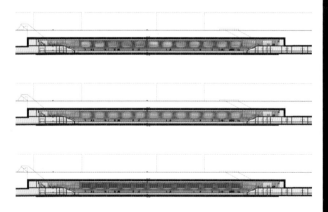

Architects: raupach architekten
Lighting designers: pfarré lighting design, d-lightvision
Designers: Design Stauss Grillmaier
Location: Versmannstraße, 20457 Hamburg, Germany
Completion: 2012
Gross floor area: 2,300 m²
Number of public levels: 2
Number of platforms: 1

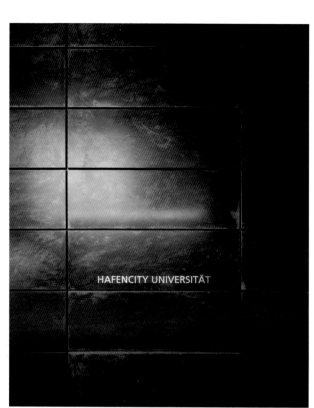

Zone 000   **Zugang nur mit gültiger Fahrkarte oder Bahnsteigkarte**   Zone 000
Entry only with valid ticket

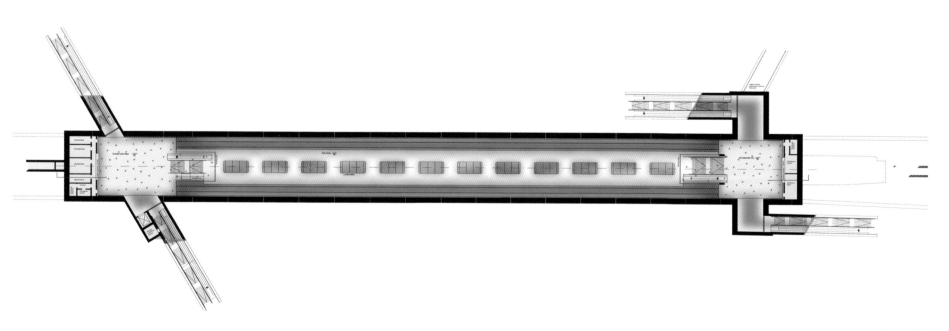

"When a train goes through a tunnel and it gets dark,
you don't throw away the ticket and jump off. You sit still and trust the engineer." –
Corrie ten Boom, Dutch watchmaker and Nazi dissident

INDEX

PICTURE CREDITS

Tom Arban 36–39 · Oliver Betz 102–105 · Patrick Bingham-Hall 144–149 · Marcus Bredt 110–113 · Till Budde 141 · Tamás Bujnovszky 14–17, 32–35, 54–57, 114–117, 166–171, 180–183 · Crossrail and Hawkins\Brown 84–87 · Marc Detiffe 154–156, 157 a.r., 172–174 · Mischa Erben 72–74, 75 a.r. · Ulla Franke 80–83 · Felix Gerlach 8–13 · Gerhard Hagen/poolima 92–97 · Roland Halbe 158–161 · Nelson Kon 176–179 · Punctum/ B. Kober 50 –53 · KVB 62–65 · Carl Lang 18–21 · Peppe Maisto / DPA / Adagp 58 –61 · Maximilian Meisse 132–135 · Arch. Moßburger ZTG 75 a.l. · Stefan Müller 118–123 · Burkhard Pahl 143 · Lukas Roth 162–165 · Daniel Rumiancew 76–79, 124–127 · Stefan Schilling 140, 142 · Hans-Christian Schink 150–153 · Markus Tollhopf 184–189 · Jens Weber 26–31 · Brent Winstone 88, 90, 91 a.r. · Simon Wood 89, 91 a.l.

All other pictures were made available by the architects.

Cover front: Tamás Bujnovszky
Cover back (from left to right, from above to below):
Stefan Schilling, Tamás Bujnovszky, Tamás Bujnovszky, Tamás Bujnovszky, Hans-Christian Schink

IMPRINT

The Deutsche Nationalbibliothek lists this publication in the Deutsche Nationalbibliografie; detailed bibliographic data are available in the Internet at http://dnb.dnb.de

ISBN 978-3-03768-191-6
© 2015 by Braun Publishing AG
www.braun-publishing.ch

1st edition 2015

Selection of projects: Editorial office van Uffelen
Editorial staff and layout: Benjamin Langer, Lisa Rogers
Graphic concept: Michaela Prinz, Berlin
Reproduction: Bild1Druck GmbH, Berlin